River
of
Solace

River of Solace

Gary Lark

FLOWSTONE PRESS

River of Solace
Copyright © 2016 Gary Lark

Winner, 2016 Turtle Island Quarterly
Editor's Choice Chapbook Award

Turtle Island Quarterly sponsors the annual
Turtle Island Poetry Awards.
Awards are chosen by the editors. More information available at
http://fourdirectionpoetry.wixsite.com/turtleisland

These poems originally appeared in the following publications,
sometimes in an earlier version:
Turtle Island Quarterly: "Father's People," and "Mike"
Windfall: "Tin Roof Oysters"

In the *Mary* section her name is referred to as Mary Qa-xas (Huckleberry) Sullivan. The "Qa-xas" comes from *Coos Texts*, Vol. I, by Leo J. Frachtenberg, part of the series *Columbia University Contributions to Anthropology*, edited by Franz Boas, reprinted from the 1913 edition as the first AMS edition 1969 by AMS Press, Inc, New York, NY.

First Flowstone Press Edition, November 2016
ISBN-13 978-1-945824-04-3

Contents

Coosan Passage	1
Mary	4
Octopus Arms	6
Untethered	8
Lumber and Fish	11
Alice's Dance	13
Tracks in the Mud	17
Patterns in the Sky	19
Father's People	21
Catch Pool	23
Madness Unimaginable	25
No One Noticed	27
And Crows Hunted Lunch	29
Little Fish	31
Blow Down	34
Canned Shad	36
River of Solace	38
Tin Roof Oysters	39
Mike	40
In the Pickleweed	42

River of Solace

Coosan Passage

They came, the derelict,
the wan, an over traveled
foul smelling bunch of mongrel
European offspring,
laboring through vast dark timber
hamstrung with narrow philosophy
and looking for a meadow in which
to plant their potatoes and bigotry.
How can you tell day from night
in this field of giant trees?
Their wagons creaked and squealed
down to the river bottom
and they stood in the willows
staring at the sky.
Where had they come to?

Their black book God seemed small here
but they held on with a vise grip.
Their axes thudded and two man saws
they called misery whips ripped
open a window of light for a potato patch,
six apple trees and a few yards of oats.
Smallpox, gonorrhea, syphilis and measles
had come years before with the boats of tall sail
and crazy trappers who killed for mountains of fur
taking many Coos, Umpqua and Coquille
with a ghost sword no one could understand.

And they knew from the Indians
still living there that water was the way to travel.
They scraped out logs in bad imitations
of the native canoe, and later made flat bottomed skiffs
to ride the tide up and back, for they lived
where brackish tide and fresh river mingle,
a few miles from the bay where crabs hid
among eel grass on shallow water islands
and clams could be dug against starvation.
But it was salmon that filled their bellies.
The example of Indian drying racks
mixed with their carried knowledge of the smokehouse.

At times all the creeks were lousy with fish.
Indian built weirs herded salmon
into catch pools. The newcomers flung fish
onto the creek banks, and later into wagons,
with hands and pitchforks.
They ate them, planted them for fertilizer,
dried them, smoked them, made stew
of fish and potatoes and wild onion.
They survived, mostly.

They had considered themselves tame people
coming from the east and the east of that
with a mind set up by reason and religion
to be captains of creation; they had thrust

themselves into a wild they intended to shape
but it was shaping them. They learned from the heathen,
who for thousands of years had learned from bear
and elk and raven and the seething tides,
from the vast life giving sea and seasons
among plants and soil and wind,
to live in this fecund wilderness.
The Indian might plant hazel nuts
or set fire to a hillside so the huckleberry,
blackcap raspberry, thimbleberry,
gooseberry, dewberry and salal
would feed them for a generation.
What the newcomers saw
were barbarians cast somewhere
outside the gates of salvation.
But the gates weren't closed
to marrying one another.

Mary

At first it sounded like a cougar
caught in a trap, but as it went on
it oscillated between a high, wavering shrill
and a grinding, guttural wail tearing the air.
It went on for three days
before the man went down the mile
to Cutbank Slough to investigate.
Mary Qa-xas (Huckleberry) Sullivan
sat in the long grass keening and rocking,
her voice sailing out over the river and across the bay.
Bill Sullivan sat among the firewood
out back staring at the sky.
Bill said her family and most of her tribe
had been killed by a bunch of miners down south
where a little gold in the bottom of a pan
and a good supply of whiskey had caused madness.
Mary wanted to go with her family.
She wouldn't eat or enter the house.
The woman dug some iris bulbs
that had come all the way from Illinois
and she and the daughter and little boy
took them down to Mary
explaining what they were
and Bill saying a native name.
Mary stared at the bulbs and people
as if from another planet.
Some days later silence came back
and Mary was still alive.

A few years after that soldiers came
and herded the tribes up the coast to a reservation,
where they were supposed to become farmers
and live like people in Yorkshire.
Their vast knowledge withered.
Some had stayed in the shadows;
some, like Mary, lived on to see the invasion
complete; some took to whiskey and oblivion.
They were amazed that a people so inept
and bizarre could displace them.
There lived among a few the memory
of a world where there were so many loons,
grebe, gulls, swans, geese, mallards, wigeons,
teal, scaup, canvasback, goldeneyes, buffleheads,
scoters, mergansers and ruddy ducks that canoes
had to push them aside to travel
on waterways that roiled with candlefish,
salmon, steelhead, herring, lingcod,
snapper, flounder, greenling and perch.
Boundless acres of clam and mussel
stretched into the infinite past.
Heron fished the shallows
and blazing white egrets adorned the trees
along miles of bay. Cormorants dried their wings
perched on trees and snags, spirits who knew
both sides of the face of water.
In the winter, when the rain drummed on cedar planks
and the wind sang its long song, Raven told of the time
when Seal Woman married a man from the village
and their children had webbed fingers and toes.

Octopus Arms

It wasn't gold, it was the trees.
White people seemed to spill from everywhere.
They came in little bunches in sea going ships,
over the mountains and down rivers.
They brought their iron tools, their cows,
their language and booze.
They built taverns and temples
and shacks strung along the bay.
Up a little valley a waterwheel
turned a drum with a belt
or cogwheel that meshed in a gear
that drove a saw blade up and down
laying slabs of fir and cedar
on the mossy ground.
Teams of oxen pulled logs down
to waterways. Log rafts were floated
down to mill sites. They cut and cut some more.
There was an endless supply of trees.

The land was warped and creased,
wrinkled so that traversing it was an ordeal.
There were game trails, and Indian trails
that ran the ridge tops then dropped down
to fishing camps or elk meadows
lush with chest high grass
and camas bulbs to be dug,
cattail pollen flour to gather;

the arching night sky
wheeled creation from season to season
and the songs of all the creatures
who lived among the folds and creeks
that spelled this green Eden
awaited the determined picks and shovels,
the dynamite and horse drawn graders
pushing little roads out from the creek bottoms
like octopus arms getting a purchase on the land.

Gold diggers in California
had attracted people to take advantage of them,
and more to take advantage of those
until there was a powerful need for lumber.
There were homes, stores, hotels and wharves,
warehouses and whorehouses to be built,
so the little mills turned into bigger ones
powered by steam and muscle.
Immigrants and drifters lined up
to push lumber from here to there,
stack it on the docks, load the ships.
Splash dams held acres of logs
that when released rushed downstream
to saws and sailing ships and markets
in San Francisco.

Untethered

A night breeze blew down river
and was caught in a back swirl of the sea wind
when Wiggins came in on a tired gelding.
He was Civil War scarred inside and out
and had meandered from Missouri
to Santa Fe, along the dry trails to California,
spent a few years there surviving on day labor,
watching the play of gold fever
and early commerce develop: mom and pop stores,
tents selling a wagonload of picks and shovels,
guaranteed-not-to-fail sluices and maps
that would take you right to creeks lined with gold.
There was too much frenzy in town,
and even though he liked the foothills
he wasn't ready for farming.
So he moved on.

It was the graceful lines of sailing ships
that lured him to the docks.
Wiggins went to work for a shipbuilder
on the north bayfront.
This was as far from the seats of power,
the scarred face of Virginia,
the pretensions of Baltimore,
as he could get. The memory
of rich lords and ladies
sitting on a hillside overlooking a battlefield

haunted him as much as the wagons
filled with body parts and the moaning
cacophony of the wounded.

Wiggins was sober, paid attention
and soon was running a crew
of draggled shipwrights.
As a Kentucky boy he had dreamed
of the sea. On off days he would sit on a bluff
and stare at the vastness stretching out beyond
everything in his past, the known
tethered to the land, twisted in a growing story.
Beyond, the sea undulated like something alive.
He collected this-and-that lumber
as he learned shipbuilding
and built a scaled down version
of the last ships of sail.
It took him six years.
He also learned to sail by making trips
down and up the coast.

Then steam took over.
There was wood to burn.
The new power that drifted in from the east
was produced by a boiler, pressure
and a stoked fire.

Ships became less sleek, more useful.
They could haul more.
You didn't have to depend on the wind.
You didn't have to know how to run the sails.
Boats on the river became small steamers.
Paddlewheels turned like they did on the Ohio.
Screw-turn propellers would replace those.
There was no stopping progress.

When Wiggins practiced on the bay,
sailing single in high wind and low,
he saw faces among the trees
and rocks, watching.
When he looked directly at them
they faded, but the eyes stayed in his mind.
The displaced and dispossessed,
ten thousand years of souls stared
over the tide flats, out of the trees
along the river. He decided it was time.
On a June morning, with crude charts
and a pile of stories he sailed across the bar
and never returned. Some said he made Hawaii,
some said an unnamed island where people
lived the old way, with no need for steam boats,
cotton gins or cannon balls. Some heard
he lived on the Mexican coast with a senorita
who owned a mescal factory.
Some said he went down six days out.

Lumber and Fish

And there were fish to be sold.
Salmon packed in boxes,
iced, salted, smoked and canned,
shipped by wagon, ship, and train
when rails came to the edge of Manifest Destiny
bringing would-be tycoons and miscreants,
people with no place to go,
and those who needed a place
as far from everywhere else as they could get.
Scots-Irish, Finns, Norwegians and Swedes
built houses on the denuded hills.
Clusters of Germans and failed farmers
came looking for any job there was.
They lumbered, fished, cut fish
or sold beer to the ones who did.
Gillnets were stretched across streams
taking all the big fish. Seiners dragged the ocean
between the bay and the horizon.
Markets in Chicago and Saint Louis
Pittsburgh and New York gobbled
the fat pink fish and asked for more.

Lumber barons trickled in from Minnesota,
Wisconsin, Maine and the pine country
of the South. These huge trees would last forever.
The country would grow forever.
The fish would last forever.
And even if they wouldn't a fellow could make

a pile of money in a matter of a few years.
And a few did. The rest worked for wages.
Even when the stock market took a dive
there were houses to build.
Hell, things might slow up for a few months
but you couldn't stop this bucking bronco
from fulfilling its God given destiny.

Lumber and fish brought workers.
Workers needed food.
Salt marshes were diked, sloughs channeled,
pastures and farms edged into forest and meadow.
Small steamboats ran mail and supplies
up the river, bringing back milk and produce.
A creamery, a cheese maker, a grocer
could make a living.

Alice's Dance

Jimmy Longtoes Johnson
sat against the building,
feeling the rough boards on his back.
He tipped the bottle,
squinted into the rain.
"What we see is edges
but ain't no edges there.
Raven knows that.
Turtle knows that.
Octopus Lady knows that.
But people, they're thick headed,
got notions piled on top of notions
then they write it down
and think they're real."
It was a month of rain.
A winter where it rained every day.
A singing rain that ran through every crack
and down every boardwalk plank,
down runnels in the mudflats
to sweeten the bay.
"I am the rain," Jimmy said, "I am the tree,
I am the skin that ain't no skin at all."
He pitched the bottle at a feather
floating in the gray between day and night.

Alice Longworth saw the bottle
spin out between the buildings.
She had been raised among this mixed lot of people

and knew when to fear and when to not.
Jimmy was one of the old ones
who talked nonsense and survived
who knows how, running the docks
and talking to himself.
She had a little distance now,
back from her freshman year
at the Methodist college upstate.
Another year and she would qualify to teach
if that's what she wanted to do.
She knows she was sent there
to look for a husband,
someone with better prospects
than the bay lads.
Though, having one of the rough scalawags
who worked ten hour shifts at her father's mill
sitting next to her at dinner did make her smile.

The Methodists weren't as bad as some
when it came to dancing, and Alice loved dancing.
At school they had several formals
during the year, part of the program
to make upstanding citizens out of them,
at least learn the façade.
Some of her friends would dance
at the pavilion to new tunes someone knew.
But there was nothing like the abandon

she felt when on a close winter night
Clay Thompson got his fiddle out
and Ryan Calhoun started on his guitar,
and people joined in with instruments
kept from dampness and ruin
with fervent attention,
playing until no dancer was left standing.
There was a sweet spot in the evening
when the musicians were warmed up
and liquored up just enough
that the dancing was perfect
Alice would spin and reel
with any and all available.

The next day her mother would give her the old lecture,
"You need to be an example. You're special.
Your father employs over a hundred men
and you need to be careful not to lead them on.
Think of your future."
Alice came close to marrying a college boy.
Brought him home, walked the beach with him,
saw how apples and oranges he was to the place
and left him at college when she came home
to start teaching in the elementary school.
She needed the sea mist, the rain, the flood tides,
the startling freshness of false spring in February,
the smell of fish and mudflats, the taste of smelt

dipped from the waves. She would be home nowhere else.
Now, her mother worried Alice would be an old maid.
But there was a sawyer who worked at a mill,
not her father's, south of town that danced just right.
He didn't push or pull, didn't drink till he stumbled,
touched her as if she were perfect.
She would try to live up to that touch.

Tracks in the Mud

Alice taught for thirty-four years.
She and Carl Larsen saw electricity, radios,
automobiles and refrigerators
become common as boots.
She also saw the effects
of a twisting economy when scraggly children
came to school not having breakfast,
and maybe a potato or a hunk of dried fish for lunch.
When the price of lumber dropped below cost
men were laid off, ships didn't run
and rail cars were left empty on a siding.
A shuttered mill could be bought by
out of state companies with deep pockets
and bean counters who would never see the trees they owned.
Some years the fish runs didn't come.

Alice saw some of her kids climb on trains
and head for the other side of the world.
A World War they would call it, an echoing voice
across such a distance that it was barely real.
The government built and ran spruce mills
for airplane parts. Lumber was needed.
The bay may be an out-of-the-way place
but the world would come to it.
Ku Klux Klan rallies drew crowds,
all mixed up with war talk and Wobblies
saying men should have the right to strike,

others calling them socialists.
There was talk of an eight hour work day.
People waving the flag, saying whoever
is against the U.S. should be run out.
There was suspicion of the Catholics,
Indians, Negroes, Chinese, Japanese and Jews.
Foreigners were to be regarded as dangerous.
To which Carl concluded, "Most of us
are newcomers or their offspring.
Those that talk loudest are looking
at their own tracks in the mud."
But notices of their dead appeared in the paper.
The sons of neighbors came home gassed
and shell shocked. Amputees struggled
along the waterfront.
Everyone knew a line had been crossed.

Patterns in the Sky

Barnstormers, touring the country
came up the coast putting on a show
for any town that could pony up a few dollars.
Four biplanes roared into town,
landing one by one on a strip of sand across the bay.
Six daredevils, crazy young men, put up flyers
all over town and talked about their exploits.
They drank beer and talked.
They talked on the plank walkways.
They talked in the barbershop.
They talked local band members into playing the next day.
It was a real hullabaloo.
Word was passed quicker than gossip.
People from upriver showed up in boats.
People streamed out of the hills, from along the sloughs.
At noon, the planes came over the hill in formation,
dipped down, almost touching the water,
then went straight up and peeled away
from each other like an opening flower.
There were a lot of oohs and aahs.
There were also two young fellows passing their hats.
Nickels, quarters and dollars dropped into the hats.
It was worth it. They flew upside down.
Streamers of smoke wrote designs in the sky.
There were banners, one of which said "Hurray for the USA."
After awhile two of the planes landed and picked up the hat passers.
And amazingly, they got up on the wings and rode through the air

as easy as anything. Even upside down.
An hour of wondrous, never-before-seen stunts,
just as the handbills had said.
Then, finally, they wove a last pattern in the sky,
and in a burst of fireworks they soared north and out of sight.

There were flappers and rumble seats,
a few fishermen who made runs for Canadian hooch,
music from faraway ballrooms drifted from radios,
and bands played the Odd Fellows hall
on their way to somewhere else.
The mills ran. Lumber was shipped.
There were jobs. Shipyard money built a hospital;
a few years later a Longworth wing was added.
Another school was built. A public library.
Paving replaced the plank roads.
But the place was still guarded by abrupt hills
and twisting river valleys, keeping it isolated,
off the track of big time growth like Seattle,
San Francisco and Portland.
There were no straight roads in or out.
So all the pretensions and hoopla
that the Chamber of Commerce could muster
went unheeded by the big industries.
There were big ideas like cutting a straight road
right through the miles of hills but nobody
with money seemed interested.
It remained lumber, fish and a seam of coal.

Father's People

They lived up the rivers on patches of bottom land
and side hills growing gardens, eating venison.
Young men could start working in the woods at sixteen
earning a man's wages, hunt the clear cuts
and fish on streams where cougar and bear
were the only competitors.
The cut pushed further into the hills.
Log trucks replaced little rail spurs
hauling some of the most beautiful wood
the world ever produced to mills
by the bay. But there were places
up the shaded river reaches
where the stillness that wasn't still
and the silence that wasn't silent
crept into the listener and wrung his mind
like Monday wash. In that place of no human sound
and primeval wonder it was like standing
on God's front porch and seeing a balance
and meaning of things that couldn't be spoken.
The murmur and crash of a small river
getting bigger as it slips and carves
through stands of virgin fir,
nursed and coaxed by alder and maple
along its banks, folds of land
untroubled but by deer hooves
and marten claws, all strewn and buckled

by plate tectonics and ice-age maneuvers,
seeds and sea bringing forth the day.
The listener would know that he was blessed
by something beyond his knowing.
Sometimes he had an axe in his hand,
sometimes a fishing pole or rifle, but he knew
he needed forgiveness with every step.

Catch Pool

Native people drifted back from reservations.
The ones who eluded the soldiers
and ones hidden by friendly whites
and their descendants got by
in the strange world where people
staked out little pieces of land as their own
and danced to a tune called progress.
Nothing slowed progress like progress.
Selling stocks and bonds at a fraction of worth,
land before you owned it, banking on speculation
was the way of things until it wasn't.
For most people along the bay the Great Depression
didn't make a lot of difference. Getting by
was a way of life, so when the fat cats
went belly up folks watched and waited
for the tail end of the tidal wave to get their boots wet.
Further up the hill there was much moaning
and gnashing of teeth. The banks closed.
But the need for lumber didn't stop,
so the wheels of the money business
would soon turn again, the mills would run
and the new high school would be built.
People from Oklahoma, Arkansas, Kansas,
Nebraska, Missouri and the spillover from California
drifted in looking for jobs.
Alice heard new accents in her classroom.
Some were ill fed urchins, dressed in hand-me-down

overalls and worn shoes they would take off
because they hurt more than the cold.
She arranged for a women's group to supply lunches
for those who, despite their embarrassment,
would take the brown bags out under the roof overhang
and devour what was offered, staring through the rain.
Longshore strikes, up and down the coast,
were joined by Teamsters, and many sawmill workers
wouldn't cross picket lines. Woodworkers would strike,
shuttering mills in the Northwest, laying the groundwork
for later struggles. World War II came in like a thug
and grabbed the able-bodied of all political stripes.

Madness Unimaginable

Another batch of Alice's kids was pulled into the next war.
The world had grown smaller with radio and highway
but Europe and Asia still seemed far away.
This time there were the demons Hitler and Mussolini
menacing one part of the sphere and the blustering
empire of Japan with its murder and rape of China
that promised there would be a great cost to stop it.
Japan having the gall to attack the United States
made it plain, something terrible had come across the sea.
Every town sent their young and able into a madness
unimaginable to the fishermen, carpenters, longshoremen,
sawmill workers and lumbermen, their wives,
mothers and friends. The veterans from the first war
mostly said "Be the first one down and the last one up"
because there was no way to tell them more truth than that.
Lumbering was seen as war work like ship building
or munitions so the trees kept being cut
and the mills ran two or three shifts a day.
But when the war got up to its terrible height
there were not enough asthmatics, flatfooted,
Jehovah's Witnesses, Mennonites and older men
to keep the mills running full time
so women put on their britches and pulled,
pushed, graded, cut and stacked lumber
like they were born to it—many had grown up
on the bay or in the tree producing hills
and knew the business their daddies and brothers

brought home with the sawdust in their hair.
The war ground on, the Fourth of July fervor
as strident as usual seemed shallow
and tinny as it traversed Second Street,
turned down Longworth and back up Fourth.
The maimed trickled home, going on
as best they could; others, with hollow eyes,
sat by the fire afraid to sleep.
Many didn't come home at all.
The names Omaha Beach, Anzio, Salerno,
St. Lo, Dachau, Iwo Jima, Bataan, Saipan and Okinawa
were seared into a generation like a brand.
A few Japanese balloon bombs landed
but failed to set the vast forests ablaze.
One, however killed six at a church picnic
east of the mountains—an act of devilment
that fell from the sky like a cinder
of a fire thousands of miles away.
Japanese Americans had been corralled
in internment camps, many of them losing
everything. Such was the fear of the Yellow Peril.
The few along the bay disappeared
without much thought and the Chinese
families were under the many-eyed microscope
for the duration. But this was no San Francisco.
Surviving was the common denominator
and daily bread, or fish, was the goal.

No One Noticed

Carl died at the mill one day—
an indicator of the passing generation,
the ones who knew the bay
in the old days, when time and work
lay differently on the land.
Alice wondered why the earth didn't shake,
why nothing changed, why no one noticed
the giant crack in the universe.
Alice lived to see many of her kids
go to college on the GI Bill, others
folded back into the mill jobs
or felling, shagging and hauling
logs on rumbling trucks.
It was a time of mills running
three shifts a day, union wages,
expanding schools, movie theaters,
long sleek cars that most could afford,
dance music coming from far away,
following on the heels of the big bands,
with a city beat, enticing the young
to Portland or crazy California.
The Korean War took a bite out of the Jitterbug
but didn't kill it. Its bitterness seeped
into families like the ice at Chosin Reservoir.
There were some who wondered if this business
of saving people halfway around the world
every few years was a good idea.

But most went when called;
some of those died, some lost toes to the cold,
a few refused to go down the hill
and were not shot because their companions
stood by them. They came home,
worked in the mill and took the family
to the drive-in for hamburgers
letting their dreams float away
under the pale Korean moon.

And Crows Hunted Lunch

There were more people at Alice's funeral
than her father's, twenty two years before.
There were her students, parents of her students,
children of her students and a few old ghosts
from her father's time haunting the back pews.
The Presbyterian minister, whom she knew
more as friend and ally than spiritual advisor,
led a chorus of praise as one attendee
after another rose to tell a story.
Some fifty cars joined the procession
to the burial ground south of town.
Seagulls wheeled and crows hunted lunch
and the day went on as usual.

Big companies bought up the timber,
squeezed family owned mills
until they were ripe for the picking.
Upstream, the small outfits with pond
and wigwam burner would dry up,
sometimes selling useful machinery,
sometime not, worker's shacks then falling
to blackberries and rot. Independent cutters
and haulers, scrappers and firewood scroungers,
woodmen from birth, started working
for people they didn't know and couldn't see.
Profits dribbled out of state,
decisions were made by suits

on the advice of accountants
with an eye for Wall Street.
Machines did more of the work,
but labor strength kept good wages,
the eight hour day and forty hour week.
A community college was formed.
New handwriting appeared in the mud.

Little Fish

Someone started a coffeehouse
like one they had seen in California.
There were theater groups putting on plays
at the college and uptown.
Folk musicians drifted through town.
Ray's draft notice came on a terribly normal day.
Viet Nam had been in the news
but Ray couldn't imagine it affecting him.
It became real on the bus ride, at the cattle call
induction center, in the no-choice whirlpool
that sucked him into uniform, Basic Training,
infantry training. He felt like he was trained
for fake fights and laying in the dirt
firing at targets at Fort Lewis, for fifteen mile
marches along a dirt road. It still seemed impossible
that he was going to drop into war
when the big plane landed in the tropical heat.
They were all scared, but they were young,
at home in their bodies.
Some bristled for action, some watched
with eyes older than their faces.
Ray Cavanaugh came face-to-face with the disease
at their first inspection, in front of temporary tents,
waiting for the real show to begin.
A first lieutenant named Carver walked
down their lines showing each one a photograph.
"This is a Porsche. My Porsche. This is my wife.

I love my Porsche, do you understand?"
They answered yessir.
"I will not let you green pigs fuck up my life.
I will not let you get me killed."
Is that clear?"
Yessir.
Ray knew this man was poison.
Through the heat and rain and madness
he saw the river at home sliding into the bay,
the calm when the tide changes direction,
a cloud of egrets lifting out of the trees
sailing into the marshes and pastures
feeding on snails and frogs and little fish.
He was a little fish.
From then on he had two conflicting notions
constantly in his mind: to survive by helping
his squad to survive and hoping that when he was shot
it would be bad enough to send him home.
In the same fight where Carver was killed,
Ray was shot in the hip and through the right lung.
While he waited for the chopper,
aware of the cold rot on his feet in a morphine haze,
hearing his lung try to suck air,
Witherspoon leaned over him, "It look like you goin' home.
Look like Carver goin' home too, in a box.
Can't tell which way the bullet was goin'
but it don't matter. When you git there

kiss the ground fo me."
In Japan they said he was lucky.

The second week Ray was home
he backed over his .300 Remington with his truck.
Then broke apart his 12 gauge,
dropped the trigger housing into the bay,
smashed the .38 Colt revolver with a sledgehammer
until it was useless. He beat the little .22
against a tree, splintering the stock
and gave the barrel the truck treatment.
Then he went fishing.
Every day he went to the river
where the motion inside the motion
soothed him. Only in that motion
was there the stillness he was looking for.
Some nights you could hear the purr of his outboard
crossing the pearled reflection of moon
as he trolled for striped bass.
He trolled until he stopped expecting sniper fire
and the concussion of a trailside, booby-trapped shell
no longer arrived on a gust of wind.
Ray got a job cleaning the elementary school
afternoons and evenings, leaving mornings
for the river. There was a teacher there
who greeted him every day with a shy warmth.
She was not exactly pretty but her smile
was like the sun breaking through a gray horizon.

Blow Down

A few years before, a mammoth storm
had blown down miles of trees
and companies started to ship raw logs
to buyers overseas.
They got used to it: lower labor costs and eager buyers.
Lumber mills, the plywood mill and paper mill ran apace.
There was talk of building a new school or two.
The high school football team competed for titles.
Taxes kept up with expanding neighborhoods.
The war ended with a distant gasp
and the Ruggles Family Circus came to town.
Companies cut faster than trees grow,
coming to rely on National and State forests
for a continuing supply, until the rules changed.
Protection for endangered species, overcutting,
automation and selling unprocessed logs
fell like an axe on this lumbering town.
Mills shut down. Money dried up or left town.
Thousands were thrown out of work.
Blame the spotted owl, the marbled murrelet,
the dwindling salmon and cutthroat trout,
blame the politicians in the capital,
(politicians blamed whatever was handy)
but blame didn't pay the mortgage.
Cars and trucks and trailers were packed,
For Sale signs were planted in front yards,
a desperate migration fanned out to Seattle,

California, oil fields, family in Arkansas,
fishing or lumbering in Alaska, wherever there might be a job.
But manual labor jobs were withering on the industrial vine.
Another invisible line had been crossed.

Canned Shad

Ray and Lisa felt like they were holding on
to an upturned hull, riding out the storm.
Lisa had been there long enough
that others were let go first
but Ray was cut back to halftime
even though the work remained the same.
Friends and colleagues went to places
where new wave electronics supplied the jobs.
The high school dropped into a lower division.
Ray's brined, lightly smoked, canned shad
became going away gifts rather than holiday fare.
Bitterness oozed from proud families,
once owners of new trucks that hard work provided.
Bumper stickers spoke their consternation:
"Save a logger, eat a spotted owl,"
"Sierra Club kiss my axe."
Some shopped late so their food stamps
wouldn't be seen by many.

Lisa's classroom turned from a chaotic thirty-six
to seventeen. Children dropped out of sight
as families left town. Stores closed, restaurants
dried up, thrift stores became mainstream.
Those who stayed hunkered down, weathering the storm.
Salmon harvests declined, canneries shut,
ocean trawlers for sale at a tenth their worth,
crabbers, shrimpers and tuna boats

rode the waves of fluctuating stocks.
People stoked the woodstove, picked mushrooms,
fished off the rocks, picked fern, moss and mistletoe
for florists upstate, tended the garden
and a few guarded a patch of marijuana.
Ships were still loaded with unprocessed logs
and one mill still operated. Small trees
were chipped and the fiber glued into a sheet.
Over the hills, stretching out from the bay,
among the stump ranches, folks pastured a beef cow
or a skein of dairy goats around the big stumps
left in one decade or another by the timber companies,
particularly in those times and places
before they were made to replant
viable wood bearing trees instead of leaving
that business to God's handmaiden, chance.
Blackberry, salal, foxglove, huckleberry
and every other kind of brush imaginable
took the plentiful rain and spread wherever
there wasn't dense forest to crowd out the sun.

River of Solace

Days became years. Lisa saw some of her kids
recruited for wars in Iraq and Afghanistan.
Poverty and the dearth of opportunity
made the advertising look good
and like poor everywhere they put on the uniform
and did the work that old rich men
asked them to do. Shell shock became PTSD.
There was no draft but the advertising was relentless.
More and more women joined.
The amount of suicide and sexual assault was suppressed
for a while, but you can't keep the lid on trauma.
Another generation came back to the bay
needing the river to wash over them
and the quiet tidal surge to flood
their stronghold of nightmares.

Tin Roof Oysters

Down along Crab Flats Lonnie Henderson
has a little fire going. There's a bushel of oysters,
a case of beer. He puts a piece of tin roofing
over a portion of the fire, spreads oysters on top
and flops bay soaked burlap over them.
Folks arrive in singles and bunches.
Lapping water absorbs the afternoon gray.
Four people off to the side pass a joint.
Crab Flats wanders along a shell road
about six feet above high tide,
interrupted by stone outcrops and salal.
A row of weathered houses hunkers there,
patched together by people who get by
on what can be gleaned from bay and society,
day to day, enough if you don't want too much.
Pies and salads arrive. A bucket of mussels
joins the oysters. A couple of round
brown loaves of still warm bread
gets some attention.
There's talk of salvage, cutting firewood,
seasonal work for the BLM, pros and cons
of the Indian casino. Someone says they should
start growing pearls after a seed pearl is found.
A longshoreman starts strumming a guitar,
a wildlife biologist begins to sing along.
The oysters are hot in their salty juices
and the bell buoy clangs in the rocking waves
as fog starts to creep in.

Mike

Everyone along the bay knows Mike's truck,
the old blue Chevy with the drab aluminum camper shell,
but what is distinctive is the splendid canoe on top.
He built it in a friend's garage twelve years ago
replacing one he built forty years ago.
The cedar strip marvel took two years,
every detail perfect.
Mike is somewhere between seventy and a hundred,
five foot seven with his boots on, with the face
of a wizened child that had been put, top to bottom, in a vise.
Growing up on the bay he swam
in the sewer runoff slough water,
gathered crab and clams by traversing the currents
on a slab of bark, learned every nook and creek
along the miles of shoreline.
He lives half the time out of his truck
and the other half wherever there is a friend
and shelter. He keeps a smoke house going
at one of those places, filled, depending on the season,
with salmon, steelhead or lingcod.
He delivers to his regular customers
and they're grateful. He has never paid taxes,
not out of ideology, just doesn't exist in that world.
One of the things he enjoys most is to pull alongside
a multi-thousand dollar boat, rigged out with the best gear,
with two large Chinook laying in the bottom of his canoe
and ask about the fishing.

His favorite though, is navigating up a small stream
with the incoming tide when the fall Chinook are running—
at one with the water, the fish and the season,
the tall salt-marsh grass waving and leaning with the wind,
the Sitka spruce holding the world together
and the fish rising in circles all around him.

In the Pickleweed

Melissa Kendrick measures and records data,
walking the marsh, monitoring acid levels,
dissolved oxygen, tracing nitrogen,
looking for changes and trends in runoff
from farms and development,
checking micro-life in the layers of flood debris,
humus, bark and decaying plants.
Part of an ongoing study of the bay
started in the time of her grandparents,
she is one of the current crop of graduate students
studying the estuary and the ocean nearby.
Grief and admiration stir in her belly:
grief for great salmon runs that used to boil
in every wet spot, the bird life that was,
and the despoilment that only humans know how to do;
admiration for the tenacity of the fir
and salal and huckleberry, the dogged
nature of alder nursing the next renewal,
the composting nature of the marsh.
The data shows some fish renewal
but it will never reach the fecundity
of a hundred and fifty years ago.
The wrinkled land brings second, third
and fourth growth out of the rain and death
along the denuded ridges.
Global climate change spills from the data
and no one knows how that will play out.

Will this be the place where thousands
of eco-refugees come when Midwest aquifers dry,
when Phoenix and Las Vegas collapse?
She imagines heavy drought years
where streams they study stop flowing,
or wicked storms flood everything.
But today there is a quiet on the slough
that folds over her. The tide presses
into the pickleweed at her feet,
a harbor seal surfaces and makes eye contact,
cormorants fish from a cluster of old pilings.
A great wheel turns here
and she feels privileged to see it.

About the Author

Gary Lark's work includes *In the House of Memory* (BatCat Press, 2016), *Without a Map* (Wellstone Press, 2013), *Getting By* (Winner of the Holland Prize from Logan House Press, 2009), and three chapbooks. His work has appeared in *Beloit Poetry Journal*, *Hubbub*, *Poet Lore*, and *The Sun*. Three poems were featued on *The Writer's Almanac* with Garrison Keillor. Gary lives with his wife Dorothy in Oregon's Rogue Valley.

www.ingramcontent.com/pod-product-compliance
Lightning Source LLC
Chambersburg PA
CBHW070039070426
42449CB00012BA/3092